The New Land

A First Year on the Prairie

written by Marilynn Reynolds

illustrated by Stephen McCallum

ORCA BOOK PUBLISHERS

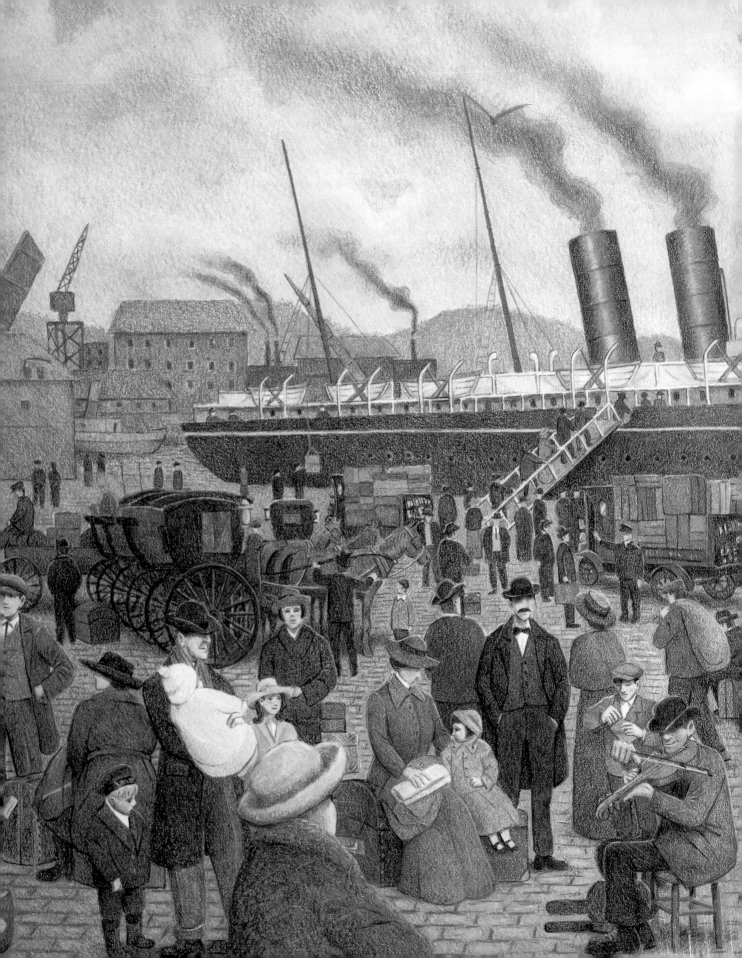

In memory of my pioneer grandparents Alice and John Lloyd.
M.R.
For my grandparents who came to the new land.
S.M.

ONE springtime when the apple trees were in bloom, Father, Mother, John and little Annie left the old country to find a home in the new world.

They said goodbye to the castles and the cottages. Goodbye to the crowded cities and the little farms. Goodbye to the factories and the apple trees. Goodbye to everything they knew.

Then they set sail across the ocean.

For fourteen days and fourteen nights they sailed. The water was so rough they were seasick every day of the voyage.

When the boat reached the new country, the family boarded a train that chugged past farms and villages, along the shores of lakes, down into valleys and up over hills. For days it rattled along, until it came to the end of the railway track in the middle of the great prairie and it could go no farther.

At the end of the rail stood a town where Father bought a wagon. He loaded it with supplies: a pick and shovel, a lantern, blankets, nails, a tin kettle, cooking pots, a stove and sacks of food.

At the livery stable he bought a team of shorthorn oxen named Big Red and Mike. He yoked them together and hitched them to the wagon. The canvas top of the wagon billowed out behind them as the oxen slowly pulled the family over the flat land toward their new home.

The family had never seen anything as wonderful as the prairie. Short green grass, as thick as a carpet, stretched out before them like the ocean they had crossed. When the wind blew, the grass swelled like the waves of the sea.

When John looked down, he saw that the grass was laced with thousands of buffalo tracks. Sometimes the wagon passed over trails made by the Indians.

As the wagon moved along, meadowlarks nesting in the grass sang their songs and gophers popped out of their holes to take a look at the new people.

Once an antelope darted in front of the oxen, but Big Red and his smaller partner, Mike, never turned their heavy heads. Slowly, slowly they pulled the wagon — as strong as a team of horses, but no faster than a man could walk.

Three days later they came to an iron stake that marked the homestead. Mother and Father climbed down from the wagon. Their long journey was over. They were standing on their own land at last.

The first night on their homestead they camped in a field of wildflowers. Because there were no trees for firewood, Mother and John gathered dry buffalo chips to burn in the campfire. After supper they huddled around the warm embers, and when it got dark, they slept together by the wagon.

Next morning Father searched for water. Father was a diviner. He cut a forked willow branch from the brush that grew down by the slough, and he strode up and down holding the branch out in front of him. Suddenly Father stopped. He felt a pull on the branch that meant there was water under the ground.

Father began to dig a well. He dug for hours, using a pail to carry the dirt out of the hole. When the hole was deep, he built a ladder so that he could climb down. At the end of the day he struck water, and when he crawled up out of the well, all wet and muddy, the family ran to him. They hugged each other and danced around in a circle on their new land.

The next job was to build a house. Father drove Big Red and Mike into town for supplies. The oxen moved as slowly as snails, and when they were tired, they lay down to rest and wouldn't get up until they felt like moving again. Six days later they came home with a load of lumber for the new house.

With the lumber, Father and Mother built a wooden shack eight paces wide and six paces deep. The house had one door and four small windows.

Father cut slabs of sod from the prairie grass, and the family stacked them in a double row around the outside of the wooden house right up to the eaves to keep it warm. They laid the sod on top of the roof, and when their house was finished, they built a sod barn for the animals.

At the end of the summer Father drove the oxen twenty miles to a valley of trees. They were gone for three days, but they returned with a wagon full of poplar poles. Father stacked them in the yard like a giant teepee. When the poles dried out, he would cut them into logs to burn in the stove and keep the sod house warm.

Soon autumn came to the prairie. The nights grew cold and the prairie grass turned brown. Father hitched Big Red and Mike to the plough, and they broke the land in a wide fireguard around the house and barn to protect the homestead from prairie fires.

Father mowed prairie grass for the oxen to eat during the coming winter. Then he tied a rope from the door of the sod house down to the barn door so that in the very worst snowstorms, he could find his way to the barn to feed the animals.

When the first snowflakes fell on the prairie, the family was ready for winter in its new home. Inside the sod house Mother hung blankets from the ceiling to divide the house into rooms. On the walls she arranged the precious photographs of their families that they had brought all the way from the old country.

During the cold dark winter they spent their time around the glowing stove. Outside, they could hear the coyotes calling to one another. By the light of a single lantern they read, played cards and wrote letters to their friends back home. Often they were homesick.

But springtime came back to the prairie. The snow melted and purple crocuses sprang up in the green grass. Overhead, wild geese flew north to their nesting ground and meadowlarks warbled songs that were answered by their mates hidden in the grass.

In the bright sunshine Father broke the land with a walking plough and planted his first field of wheat. Mother and John planted a garden of potatoes, peas, onions, turnips and beans.

And they planted apple trees — strong hardy young apple trees that could grow in the new land. Apple trees that would bloom every spring just like the trees they had left behind.

The publisher would like to acknowledge the ongoing financial support
of the Canada Council, the Department of Canadian
Heritage and the British Columbia Ministry of Small Business, Tourism
and Culture.

Canadian Cataloguing in Publication Data
Reynolds, Marilynn, 1940–
The new land

ISBN 1-55143-069-X (bound)

1. Frontier and pioneer life—Prairie Provinces—Juvenile fiction. I.
McCallum, Stephen, 1960– II. Title.
PS8585.E973N48 1997 jC813'.54 C96–910789–7
PZ7.R33735Ne 1997

Library of Congress Catalog Card Number 96-72452

Design by Christine Toller
Printed and bound in Hong Kong

Orca Book Publishers
PO Box 5626, Station B
Victoria, BC V8R 6S4
Canada

Orca Book Publishers
PO Box 468
Custer, WA 98240-0468
USA

99 98 97   5 4 3 2 1